Colón Cemetery, Havana, Cuba

A TRAVEL PHOTO ART BOOK

LAINE CUNNINGHAM

Colón Cemetery, Havana, Cuba

A Travel Photo Art Book

Published by Sun Dogs Creations
Changing the World One Book at a Time
Print ISBN: 978-1-951389-16-1

Cover Image by Laine Cunningham
Cover Design by Angel Leya

Copyright © 2024 Laine Cunningham

All rights reserved. No part of this book may be reproduced in any form or by any means, electronic, mechanical, digital, photocopying or recording, except for the inclusion in a review, without permission in writing from the publisher.

The Colón Cemetery, with over 500 major mausoleums, holds a number of elaborate memorials. Sculptures, wrought iron borders, and cast metal doors decorate a number of the graves. Historically as well as architecturally, the site is considered one of the most important cemeteries in Latin America and the world.

Inside the walls stands the Central Chapel, which was modeled after Florence's Il Duomo. Different segments, or barracks, of burial sites organize plots based on official rank or social status. Space in Colón is so in demand that remains are removed from tombs after three years and placed in a storage building.

Step through the Romanesque main gate and wander through El Cementerio de Cristóbal Colón.

APPROACH

AWAKE

BRACE

YEARN

LAUREL

HYMN

OFFERING

GOLDEN REPOSE

RAFT

FAITHFUL

ASCEND

VISITATION

PIKE

CASTLE

INTERLUDE

PERPETUAL

RISE

STRONGHOLD

TABLEAU

WAYSTATION

COURSING

SHIELD

HERMITAGE

COMPOSURE

GERMINATE

SHEAVES

GATEHOUSE

GROTTO

REFUGE

PHOENIX

HARBOR

MESSAGE

TRANSOM

WEEP

TARRY

SOOTHE

GLORY

TITLES IN THIS SERIES

Havana, Cuba
Old Havana, Cuba
The Malecón, Havana, Cuba
Central Havana, Cuba
Vedado, Havana, Cuba
Regla, Havana, Cuba
Miramar, Havana, Cuba
Streets of Havana, Cuba
Classic Cars of Cuba
Classic Cars of Old Havana, Cuba
Classic Cars of Havana, Cuba
Spanish Colonial Havana, Cuba
Gardens of Havana, Cuba
Verge Gardens of Havana, Cuba
Cats of Havana, Cuba
Colón Cemetery, Cuba
Havana Art School

www.ingramcontent.com/pod-product-compliance
Lightning Source LLC
Chambersburg PA
CBHW040002080526
44586CB00027B/2856